The Ministry of Intercession

The Ministry of Intercession

BY F. J. HUEGEL

DIMENSION BOOKS
BETHANY FELLOWSHIP, INC.
Minneapolis, Minnesota

The Ministry of Intercession
by F. J. Huegel

Library of Congress Catalog Card Number 76-15861

ISBN 0-87123-365-7

Second edition 1976

DIMENSION BOOKS
Published by Bethany Fellowship, Inc.
6820 Auto Club Road, Minneapolis, Minnesota 55438

Printed in the United States of America

DEDICATION

To Iyre, John, Sharon and Mildred, faithful prayer partners over the years, I lovingly dedicate this book

TABLE OF CONTENTS

CHAPTER I

INTERCESSION, THE GREATEST OF ALL MINISTRIES

The Christian, very naturally, desires to do good. He knows that, even as his Lord who came not to be ministered unto but to minister unto others, he must serve to bless others. He longs to be of service to those in need. He remembers his Savior's word that those who abide in Him shall bear much fruit, and that in the fruit the Father is glorified.

However, he feels keenly his limitations. Perhaps he cannot go to lands where Christ his Lord is still unknown, as missionaries are wont to go. He cannot preach the gospel as preachers do. He perhaps is not in a position to give large sums to bless needy souls and to further Christian causes. He would like to be a Billy Graham and lead multitudes to Christ. But his gifts and capacities are indeed meager. He sighs in frustration. What is he to do? He remembers his Master's word that the unfruitful branch is cut off and cast into the fire, it being withered and useless. How he does long to bear much fruit that the Father might be glorified.

Little does he realize that there is a way by which he may achieve and bear fruit far beyond the possibilities of the most gifted Christian. It has never occurred to him that within his hands are the means whereby he may bless mankind as the millionaire, who gives all that he has, could never do.

Oh, that he might realize that God has placed before him an open door through which he may enter to riches greater than those of the wealthiest man on earth! Would to God that he might know that he can achieve as the most eloquent preacher, or the most gifted missionary, or the most compassionate philanthropist could never attain!

That is to say, if he should grasp what the Lord places in his hands. He may be too old in years to labor in the vineyard of his Lord. He may be crippled and unable to walk. He may be bedridden with an incurable disease. He may be in an iron lung. He may be blind, one whom others must lead. He may never have had the advantages of college or seminary training. He may never have had a course in Bible or sat under some renowned teacher of the Word. He may dwell in some insignificant village and be a nobody, as to the church. He may have come to the end of the road and have been laid aside as a worn out and useless life, a burden to others. Still he may achieve as only an apostle could.

You may think that I am painting an impossible picture. You laugh at what you feel could never come to pass. You may say to yourself, "This man is mad." You may think, if ever a writer was off the beam, it is this one.

Now I wish to say that if ever as a Christian author I am securely on the beam it is now. If ever I was on unshakeable ground it is now. I stoutly affirm that if ever I may have been sure that God was speaking through me, it is now. If I should say thus saith the Lord as the prophets of old were wont to say, no one could laugh at me. No one could say, "You are crazy." I have God's Holy Word to substantiate what I am saying. In a sense, what I am saying is nothing more nor less than God's own word. It is He who says it. I am only affirming what the King of kings and Lord of lords declares to be true.

What is it now that is so mighty to achieve for the good of mankind? What is the magic means by which immeasurable fruit may be borne? What is this miracle-working power which far outdistances all other ministries? What is this instrument for good which, in comparison, puts all other means in a secondary role?

The answer is found here and there, and most everywhere, across the pages of the sacred word of the Scriptures. The answer is found on the lips of Jesus our Lord. The answer is found in John's Gospel, chapter 15, where the Master speaks of the Christian's need of bearing fruit, saying: "I am the vine, ye are the branches: He that abideth in me, and I in him, the same bringeth forth much fruit: for without me ye can do nothing." He adds a word regarding the means by which much fruit may be borne. It is prayer. However, I shall be using the word intercession as having an emphasis which the word prayer does not have—namely, supplication in behalf of others. Now hear what the Master says: "If ye abide in me, and my words abide in you, ye shall ask what ye will, and it shall be done unto you.''

Here our Lord and Savior Jesus Christ opens the door which leads to the most fruitful ministry of all the ministries, whether it be giving or serving or preaching.

The importance of this ministry is clear to all who love truth: *intercession provides the necessary basis for God to work.* This ministry, in comparison, is greater than all others as God is greater than man. It is one thing for me to work, it is another for God to work. It is not folly to say that without intercession, God cannot work the things He wishes to do in the salvation of sinful men. God limits Himself to our intercessions. We read that *in His own home town,* Jesus, who had healed lepers, opened the eyes of the blind, restored to health and happiness every form of human ills and suffering, and raised one from the dead (one who already stank), could not do mighty works because of the unbelief of the people. Where there is no intercession there is unbelief.

If I really believed the promises of God, as found in Holy Writ, I would enter upon the ministry of intercession at once. I would give it first place in the activities of the day. I would find time though it should mean violence—that is, a severe denial of self.

I do not think it would be a lack of modesty for me to say that what I am affirming grows out of fifty years of missionary service in many lands. I have also taught theology in the Union Seminary of Mexico City.

But more than this, I have just emerged from a great trial which for almost three years signified a thousand deaths. We are to count it joy when we are severely tempted in diversified forms. As it was with Job, the gold comes forth free from all alloys. A fellow worker, pastor of a Methodist Church in Mexico City, said to me: "Something special must come out of your suffering." This is it. I could do nothing but pray for nigh unto three years. Then came the promise found in Romans (16:20), "The God of peace shall bruise Satan under your feet shortly." To say that this was precious is putting it mildly. It was done. My every breath now is praise.

Intercession shall have first place. It is not a simple or easy matter. It means the Cross, a participation in the Savior's sufferings. But it also means a grand enrichment and glory beyond words to describe and blessings untold for others.

CHAPTER II

WE OUGHT ALWAYS TO PRAY

In the parable of the widow who cried unto the unjust judge, saying, "Avenge me of mine adversary" (Luke 18:2-3), we have the admonition from the Savior's lips—namely, that men ought always to pray and not to faint. The natural reaction to this is that it is not possible. No one can pray without ceasing. Who could possibly be on his knees day and night crying unto God?

What seems to be an absurd admonition becomes an easy and unspeakably delightful exercise when we take into account the glory of the Christian's position before God. Here praying without ceasing becomes a thing as natural as breathing, something which springs from the very nature of things. It is like a bird on the wing or the crying of a babe for its mother's milk.

Now, what is this position which makes intercession so easy and natural? It appears in the Lord's high priestly prayer as it is in John's Gospel, chapter 17, verse 24: "Father, I will that they also, whom thou hast given me, be with me where I am, that they may behold my glory, which thou hast given me: for thou lovedst me before the foundation of the world." We must not say that such glory is not for the Christian until he is called home and enters through the pearly gates into the Holy City, the New Jerusalem; that such glory can never be achieved here below in this sin-cursed world.

For a further study of the Lord's words makes it clear that He is speaking of the Christian's position in this old world where sorrow and misery and death hold sway. We read it in chapter 15 of John's Gospel where the Master bids us to abide in Him as a branch in the vine. He in us and we in Him; one with Him in a union that brings Him, as one writer puts it, nearer than hands and feet. It is such a oneness that constitutes Christ the soul of our soul, the very substance of our life. Did not the Lord say that without Him we could do nothing? "I in them and thou in me, that they may be made perfect in one; and that the world may know that thou hast sent me, and hast loved them, as thou hast loved me" (John 15:23).

But it is not until we come to St. Paul's epistles that we see what this union with Christ really means. It runs through the writings of Paul as a golden thread. It is the very heart of his concept of the Christian life. Does he not say, writing to the Philippians, that Christ is our life and that when He shall appear we shall appear with Him in glory? Paul counted all things but loss, but dung, that he might win Christ and be found in Him sharing with Him the power of His resurrection and the fellowship of His sufferings, being made conformable unto His death (Phil. 3:8-10).

A close look into the epistles of this foremost interpreter, the chief among the apostles, this one who was caught up into the third heaven where he heard things unspeakable which, he felt, he dared not utter; I repeat, a close look into the writings of Paul brings to light a breathtaking fact. It is that the Christian shares with his Savior, Christ Jesus, the Lord, the very same position that He occupies.

Christ was crucified. The Christian shares with Him His Cross. "I have been crucified together with Christ, nevertheless I live, yet not I, but Christ liveth in me, and the life which I now live in the flesh I live by the faith of the Son of God, who loved me and gave himself for me" (Gal. 2:20). You do not mean to say that I (poor little me) am to look upon myself in the same manner? You surely do not expect me to occupy such a position? Paul's answer is that they that are Christ's have crucified the flesh with its affections and lusts (Gal. 5:24).

Christ died. The Christian shares with His Lord His death. "Ye died and your life is hid with Christ in God" (Col. 3:3), which is a more correct rendering of the verse than as we have it in the King James Version.

"But you do not expect me who loves life and delights in all good things of earth, to look upon myself in such a fashion," you reply. I thought you would say that. But the Apostle commands you to do so. "Reckon ye also yourselves to be dead, indeed, unto sin, but alive unto God" (Rom. 6:11). Some of you may be saying, "Horrors, this is not the Christian life as it is being lived today. Give me a sunny Christianity, not one of cloisters and tombs." Just a moment. We have not yet finished with Paul's affirmations regarding the Christian life.

Christ arose from the tomb. When He arose, you, according to the plan of God, also arose. "Even when we were dead in sins hath he [God] quickened us together with Christ." "Ye are risen with him [Christ]," writes Paul to the Colossian Christians. "God who is rich in mercy," writes Paul to the saints at Ephesus, "for his great love wherewith he loved us, hath quickened us together with Christ and hath raised us up together." Perhaps you are holding your breath, amazed, if not overcome, by such sublime heights which you may never have dreamed were yours. You, no doubt, have lived under the delusion that it was up to you to imitate Christ, follow His example as best you could. But wait, there is more.

Christ ascended. You too have ascended. You were not only raised up; you were made to sit together with Christ in heavenly places. (See Ephesians 2:6.) We are even told that, having received the gift of righteousness through faith, we shall reign in life by one Jesus Christ. Please note, "reign in life." Paul does not say "in heaven after death." No, he says, now, right where you are, you are to reign by one Jesus Christ.

I hope you haven't shrugged off this tremendous truth, saying, "Pshaw, this is not the Christian life as it is lived today." You no doubt are right. But it is the Christian life as the Bible teaches it and as the early Christians lived it.

Now I come to the point of the chapter: We ought always to pray. Prayer is the Christian's life. We are to pray without ceasing as our Lord would have us do. In this lofty position of identification with Christ, prayer is as natural as breathing. Here we breathe the very atmosphere of heaven. "Our conversation," writes Paul to the Philippians," is in heaven; from whence also we look also for the Saviour, the Lord Jesus Christ: who shall change our vile body, that it may be fashioned like unto his glorious body, according to the working whereby he is able even to subdue all things unto himself" (Phil. 3:20-21).

I repeat, in this glorious position, which is the rightful heritage of Christians, prayer, intercession, as I propose in these chapters, becomes as easy and natural as the cry of a baby for its mother's milk, if you will pardon the repetition. All that is lacking is faith to make it real.

We can no more stop interceding than we can put an end to the beating of our heart. We can no more lay aside communion with our Lord than we can end communion with someone dearly beloved here upon earth. We keep up a stream of secret conversation with our blessed and infinitely adorable Lord no matter what our state or occupation may be. The pilot at the plane's controls, the wife about her household duties, the athlete in the midst of his sport, the preacher as he works on next Sunday's sermon, the farmer as he plows his field, the merchant as he plies his trade, the student as he digs into his lessons, the lover as he writes to the lovely maid of his dreams—one and all may take immeasurable delight in fellowship with their Lord. They may find joy unspeakable in secret prayer. They pray as Jesus would have it, without ceasing.

CHAPTER III

CHRIST OUR LORD INTERCEDES

As we turn to the epistle to the Romans we discover an amazing thing—namely, that Christ, our Lord, at the right hand of God, is occupied with the ministry of intercession. The passage is most significant. It is nothing short of a revelation. I shall quote the word (Rom. 8:33-34): "Who shall lay any thing to the charge of God's elect? It is God that justifieth. Who is he that condemneth? It is Christ that died, yea rather, that is risen again, who is even at the right hand of God, who also maketh intercession for us."

I am glad that I need not attempt to elaborate, or to pretend to throw any light of a theological nature upon this astounding fact. Paul speaks of the mystery of the gospel which was in the mind of God before the foundation of the world. That which has to do with the Savior's present ministry —now that the work of redemption has been consummated, now that He is even at the right hand of God—is yet more mysterious. We shall simply take it as it appears in the Word of God. Christ our Lord intercedes for us.

We have in the life of Christ a stirring account of the manner in which He appears as an intercessor in behalf of one of His disciples. Jesus sees Peter slipping as he bragged about his strength.

"I will go to prison for you. I will die for you."
"Peter," was the Master's reply, "before the cock
crows you will this very night, deny me thrice.
But I have prayed for you. When you are converted, confirm your brethren." What would have
become of this blustering fisherman, the Lord's
foremost disciple, if his Lord had not interceded
for him? In despair, he might have done as Judas
did. To think that there in glory at the right hand
of the Father the risen, ascended, glorified Christ
intercedes for you and me! Does it not take your
breath? Does it not fill you with joy? What would
become of us but for this?

In the same chapter we have the added revelation that the Spirit (the Holy Spirit) intercedes
for us with groanings which cannot be uttered.
Paul says that the Spirit helpeth our infirmities,
for we know not what we should pray for as we
ought (Rom. 8:26). Never are our infirmities greater than when we enter the ministry of intercession.
Our capacity to serve and bless others reaches
its highest expression here where our infirmities
are most apparent.

Here, too, we come upon mysteries too great
for our feeble minds. Why should the Holy Spirit
have to intercede for us with unutterable groanings? Though we may not understand, yet we may
rejoice with joy unspeakable and full of glory, as
Peter states in his first epistle (1:8).

This brings us to the point of the chapter. As
we enter the ministry of intercession we enter upon
a fellowship with Christ which excels all others,
whether it be preaching, or service, or any other
ministry. Furthermore, never are we in greater

harmony with the blessed Holy Spirit than when we give ourselves to intercession for others. We want to be filled with the Spirit, rivers of living waters flowing from our innermost being. But have we realized that it will mean intercession with groanings which cannot be uttered, in fellowship with the third person of the Holy Trinity?

All this is clearly manifested in the life of Praying Hyde, as he was called, of India. As a young man, fresh from seminary, he left home to take ship to India. On board, in his stateroom, he found a letter from one of the elders of the church of which his father was pastor. The letter contained a challenge, a question! Had John received the fullness of the Spirit for his ministry? Or was he trusting in his talents, his theological training? John became angry and threw the letter into the wastepaper basket. He stomped angrily out on the ship's deck. He did not like this intimation that he was not really prepared for his task. But the journey, as it was made in those days, was long, and so John had plenty of time to think it over. He reread the letter and decided to seek the Lord for an infilling of His Spirit. The result was a mighty baptism of power from on high. John decided that his ministry would be one of intercession.

He knew that he would be misunderstood, but he stuck to his purpose. The history of Hyde's ministry in India is one the most stirring accounts of missionary activities in all the annals of Christian missions. Before the Siolkot Convention (a large gathering of missionaries and pastors from all parts of India), John spent thirty days and nights in ceaseless intercession. He groaned with groanings which could not be uttered. He barely ate and slept. Ah, but the result was a glorious outpouring of the blessed Spirit of God upon pastors and missionaires, the beginning of a blessed time of revival in churches all over the land.

It was a time of great quickening, a surging of new life from heaven, and joy unspeakable. The Punjab Prayer Union was formed, as many others were drawn to the ministry of intercession. But it cost John Hyde his life. After some years, Praying Hyde returned to his home in Indiana to die. The attending physician found John's heart clear out of place. Such intercessions as John was wont to make take a heavy toll from the physical frame.

The story of the great revival that shook America in the days of Charles Finney is well known. Many pastors sigh sorrowfully and say, "Oh, for revival as in the days of the great Finney." But there was an unsung hero behind all this. It was Father Nash. Three weeks before the arrival of the revivalist, Father Nash would go to the towns and cities where Finney was booked to visit. There he would give himself to ceaseless intercession. Little wonder that the heavens were opened as Finney preached and that multitudes were brought to Christ.

A similar circumstance occurred in the days of the great Dwight Moody. The church at large owes a great debt to this apostle of evangelism. The story of those glorious days is well known. Not so well known is the story of the two women who ceased not to intercede for Moody when he was the pastor of a church which he had formed

in a humble colony of Chicago, made up largely
of urchins which he had gathered from the streets
of the colony. It irked Moody that these two women
should be praying so constantly for him. He felt
that they should intercede for the unsaved. But
they continued interceding for their pastor. The
answer came on a day when Moody was walking
on the streets of New York. He hastened to his
room at the hotel and on his knees cried out, saying: "Lord, withhold your hand or I shall die of
joy."

He soon became a world figure. He was no
longer an unknown preacher in a humble colony
of Chicago. He was now an apostle who shook the
country and on two continents led thousands to
Christ.

What did it? The intercessions of two humble
women who, as it were, besieged the throne of
grace until their pastor was endued with power
from on high.

CHAPTER IV

BINDING THE STRONG MAN

Intercession, when it is carried on in the Spirit, inevitably leads to conflict with the powers of darkness. It has been called prayer-warfare. It does seem strange that something so holy and spiritual as intercession before the throne of grace should lead to warfare with unseen spirits, the rulers of the darkness of this world. But such is the case. Any unwillingness to face this fact is to do what the ostrich does when danger appears: it buries its head in the sand.

The great apostle to the Gentiles, Saint Paul, speaks out boldly concerning prayer-warfare, declaring that we do not wrestle with flesh and blood but with powers, the rulers of the darkness of this world, spiritual wickedness in high places (Eph. 6:10-18). We are so prone to forget the fact that our real conflict is not on material ground, the visible forces of earth. It is on a higher plane, the unseen powers of hell, the satanic hosts of evil spirits which are behind all wickedness, the source from which it emanates.

Jesus our Lord is most emphatic on this subject. In Mark 3:22-27 where we have the scribes accusing our Lord of satanic powers, saying that He was casting out devils through Beelzebub the prince of devils, Jesus replies, saying, "How can Satan cast out Satan?" "If Satan," said He, "should rise up against himself and be divided, he cannot stand, but hath an end." "No man," our Lord goes on to say, "can enter in to a strong man's house, and spoil his goods, except he will first bind the strong man." In other words, Jesus was casting out devils because He had authority to bind the chief of devils, Satan himself.

Much of the Savior's time was spent in casting out evil spirits and commanding them to return no more. When He cast out the legion of demons that possessed the Gadarene, allowing them to enter the herd of swine feeding on the husks nearby, we are told that the unclean spirits pled with the Son of God, beseeching Him to please not cast them away out of the country, their final abode being the abyss of hell.

In Luke 10, where we have our Lord sending forth the seventy to prepare the way in the cities for His coming, He says upon their return, "I beheld Satan as lightning fall from heaven." The disciples were jubilant, for they found that the devils were subject unto them through the Name of Jesus. But they were admonished not to glory in this fact, but rather in the fact that their names were written in heaven. Speaking to the seventy Jesus said, "Behold, I give unto you power [authority] to tread on serpents and scorpions, and over all the power of the enemy, and nothing shall by any means hurt you."

St. John in his first epistle (3:8) tells us why the Son of God was manifested: that He might destroy the works of the devil. How difficult for this astounding revelation to enter the ears of the sophisticated age in which we live. Even among some Christians this unsavory fact would find little or no credence. However that may be, John goes on to say in the closing chapter, "The whole world lieth in wickedness." A more correct rendering of the verse in Greek would be, "The whole world lieth in the evil one."

I went to the mission field fifty years ago wholly ignorant of this fact. Had I known, and had I had in my hands (my spirit) the weapons which I now have, untold suffering would have been avoided, and a much more effective service to needy souls would have been rendered. After years of conflict, battling against heathen customs and pagan forces, it was finally revealed to me that Paul was certainly right in saying that the real conflict is not against flesh and blood, but against principalities and powers, against the rulers of the darkness of this world, against wicked spirits in high places. It was the dawn of a new day. Mountains of satanic oppression began to move. Souls were released from the enemy's wiles, and an atmosphere charged with the powers of the pit, heavy with the weight of unseen powers of darkness, grew to be crystal clear with the presence of God.

Many a preacher and many a missionary is confronted by barriers, or should I say, contrary forces which despite all his efforts and prayers, remain immovable, yea, defiant. How different all would be if the proper weapons were employed and the full force of the spiritual wealth and power which our Lord achieved on Calvary in behalf of a world cursed by the tyranny of Satan and his evil hosts, were released, brought to bear upon a seemingly impossible situation.

I have learned over the years that whenever I ceased to stand on the ground prepared for us at Calvary, the enemy would gain ground and refuse to move until there was a fresh appropriation of the victory consummated on the Cross. "The weapons of our warfare are not carnal," writes the apostle in his epistle to the Corinthians (II Cor. 10:4-5) "but mighty through God to the pulling down of strongholds: casting down imaginations, and every high thing that exalteth itself against the knowledge of God, and bringing into captivity every thought to the obedience of Christ."

I come now to the point I want to make in this chapter. I repeat what was said in the opening paragraph—namely, that intercession leads finally to a severe conflict with the powers of darkness which are behind all wickedness and also much of the seeming good that surrounds us. The enemy is very wiley and knows how to cover up his tracks and surround his works with the mask of a lovely brilliance.

As we intercede for others, for churches, for pastors, for missionaries, for the release of souls from the tyranny of evil spirits, and for such things as are laid upon our hearts, we often feel the need, as the Spirit leads, of grasping these weapons which are not carnal but mighty through God for the pulling down of strongholds of the evil one. We say to the enemy, "Hands off! Look at Calvary where you were stripped of your rights, where your head was bruised by the Son of God."

I have told this story elsewhere, but it is so

wonderfully significant that it bears a constant repetition. General Wainwright, in a concentration camp as a prisoner of the Japanese for five years, was reduced to an emaciated, utterly broken and undone figure, when a little airplane brought a colonel of the Allied Forces to the camp with the wonderfully good news that the Allies had won the war. Japan was defeated as was Germany, her ally. It was, as one may easily see, a veritable resurrection for the general. It put him, a withered, dying man, on his feet, clothed with the authority with which the gloriously good news of the victory of his own had endowed him. When the heads of the prison appeared to mock him, as was their custom, they were amazed to find the general erect, saying as one who had authority: "Sirs, I'm in charge here, these are my orders." The Japanese understood and gave way. From that hour on, Wainwright was king of the prison.

As we intercede for others, for pastors, for missionaries, for churches, for countries, for whatever the Lord may have laid upon hearts, there comes a moment when led of the Spirit, we must say to the powers of darkness, "I am in charge here. My Savior triumphed on Calvary's cross. Satan has been stripped of his authority. I give the command of faith. Hands off this soul, hands off this church, hands off this mission, hands off this land," as the case may be. Mountains of satanic oppression are cast into the sea, as the Savior said. The shout of victory is in the camp, and sorrow gives way to joy unspeakable and full of glory.

CHAPTER V

IN THE HOUSE OF GOD— INTERCESSION

Writing to Timothy, his son in the faith, Paul expresses the desire that this one so dear to him might know how to behave in the house of God. The church of the living God, the pillar and ground of truth (I Tim. 3:15), was not to be entered in a haphazard fashion. "These things," says the apostle, "write I unto thee, hoping to come unto thee shortly: but if I tarry long, that thou mightest know how thou oughtest behave thyself in . . . the church of the living God."

How very precious is Paul's admonition. We go to church. But do we know how we ought to behave ourselves? There are many ways of attending church. Perhaps it is just a habit, with nothing very deep or meaningful. We may sit there with critical eyes wondering when the preacher will end his, to us, rather dry sermon. We may even sleep a bit. Once I was preaching in a church in rural Mexico when to my surprise one of the elders went about poking with a stick those who were taking a nap. We may be sitting there thankful that Brother Jones was getting from the sermon the trimming he so needed. Some go to church because it is what is expected of them by friends and loved ones. As a boy I went to church with the family because Father, asking no questions, *took* us there, six of us.

Perhaps it is not a statement very far amiss, or ungracious, to say that there are not very many in any given congregation who go to church to worship God in spirit and in truth, knowing that, as Jesus says, "the Father seeketh such to worship him."

My point now is that there is no better place to carry on the ministry of intercession than the church, the house of God. Oh, what it would mean if we were interceding in the depths of our spirits for the worshipers and the preacher while he was preaching! One holds one's breath when one thinks of what it would mean if believers, instead of a careless drowsy worship, which falls far short of the kind which the Father seeks, were secretly interceding that the Holy Spirit might manifest Himself and do the work which it is His office to do—namely, to glorify Christ.

I recall with joy what took place in the community where I first labored as a missionary. The pastors of the different denominations banded themselves together to pray each morning at eight o'clock for the various churches of the city. How sweet it was to hear the Baptist pastor praying for the sheep of the Presbyterian flock, the Nazarene pastor praying for the sheep of the Baptist flock, and the Disciple of Christ pastor praying for the Nazarene flock. It was nothing short of a miracle. Great things were wrought as these under-shepherds of the sheep of the Chief Shepherd put aside sectarian interests to intercede for the true church, which is the Body of Christ.

In this community there was a dear old saint, Dona Panchita, who was anointed with an unusual spirit of intercession. Under this ministry she visited all the churches. It was generally known that when this woman, who lived in a constant spirit of intercession, would appear, the pastor experienced a secret joy. "Praise God, there is Dona Panchita," was the saying; "there will be a special blessing upon the flock today." Or, "Thank God, Dona Panchita is present. The Holy Spirit will be at work kindling the fires of devotion and joy and love." I can see her now, after many years, as she would sit among the congregations, her whole being wrapt in a Spirit of inspired adoration as she interceded for the flocks. It was a time of revival when Christians rejoiced with joy unspeakable and full of glory, as Peter puts it in his first epistle. Yes, and God's anointed servant, Dona Panchita, was largely responsible for it all.

There is no measuring the blessing which this sort of worshiper brings to the church. Oh, that their number might be multiplied by the thousands in times so perilous as these in which we live! Oh, that the Lord might raise up unnumbered hosts of anointed "prayer warriors" whose intercessions might usher in times of refreshing from the presence of the Lord, times of Spirit-wrought revival such as in the days of Finney or the days of Moody, or the days of Wesley!

We see it in the history of Zinzendorf, the father of the great Moravian movement. In the year 1717 the Count opened his estate to persecuted believers from all parts of Europe. The Count, a most devoted Christian, was converted as a mere boy wandering through a museum of sacred art. He came to a painting portraying the crucified Christ at the bottom of which were the words: "This I do for thee; what dost thou do for me?" He was overwhelmed with wonder and awe. Then and there he surrendered to Christ. Years later he threw open his estate, inviting Christians to come and find refuge from the storms of persecution which Protestants were suffering at the time. They came from all quarters, representing the different shades of doctrine and belief into which the evangelical family had already been divided.

Zinzendorf was deeply grieved to find that the voice of controversy was heard as these refugees aired their opinions regarding doctrines and forms of the church. The Count did so want to see them united for the purpose of missions in many lands where the gospel had not yet been preached. But in those days Protestantism was not concerned about foreign missions. The great commission, "Go ye into all the world and preach the gospel to every creature," was not paramount. It was an age of polemics and controversy over questions of doctrines and forms of worship. Foreign missions was an unknown thing. Differences of belief divided the Christian family into all but warring camps.

The Count gave himself to intercession. Whole nights were spent in a veritable agony of Spirit-inspired intercession. Others joined the Count, pleading at the throne of grace that these warring groups might be fused into one body, with foreign missions as the supreme goal of the church.

The answer came on August 14, when, at Zinzendorf's request, believers met to partake of the emblems of the Savior's broken body and blood shed for the redemption of the world. The heavens were opened and the glory of God revealed. The Holy Spirit was manifested taking the things of Christ and revealing them to the assembled believers, who unable to bear such glory were prostrate at the Savior's feet. When they arose they were a transformed people fused into one body. A passion for souls was now uppermost. They formed a prayer circle praying 24 hours of the day, different groups taking their turn so that the lamp of intercession never went out, day nor night. The result was that in 25 years one hundred missionaries went forth to distant lands to make known the love of Christ. These Moravians, as they were called, would sell themselves into slavery to reach souls for Christ, so great was their love and zeal.

Historians of church history point to Hernhut, the village where the great Count resided, and say that it was here that the great modern movement of foreign missions was born. Little wonder that the International Missionary Council should have chosen Hernhut, as was the case, for the celebration of its conference not many years ago with missionaries from all parts of the world attending. It was to Hernhut that John Wesley came after his conversion, to learn under the tutelage of Zinzendorf and the Moravian brethren. Wesley wrote home that he had found a church in which one breathed the very atmosphere of heaven.

Ah yes, it was intercession which lay at the heart of this glorious movement which ushered in the dawn of our modern age of foreign missions.

"Call unto me and I will answer thee and show thee great and mighty things which thou knowest not" (Jer. 33:3).

CHAPTER VI

INTERCESSION, A MINISTRY OF WORLD-WIDE SCOPE

As Christians, we know that we are to bear fruit, for in fruit the Father is glorified. In John 15 we have our Lord admonishing His disciples and urging them to bring forth much fruit. However, the much fruit would be possible only by abiding in Him, for without Him they were told that they could do nothing. "He that abideth in me, and I in him, the same bringeth forth much fruit. . . . If a man abide not in me, he is cast forth as a branch, and is withered; and men gather them, and cast them into the fire, and they are burned" (John 15:5, 6).

Christians often groan within themselves, frustrated and unhappy, not being able to bear fruit as they would. They feel deeply their limitations. Their scope for fruit bearing is reduced to the place in which they find themselves and the hour of the day in which they live.

Intercession opens the door for a ministry worldwide in its scope. Oh, how liberating it is. The intercessor finds a joy that is unspeakable and full of glory in being able to reach out a helping hand, via the throne of grace, to souls in distant lands. He is bound by neither time nor place.

Our Lord in His talk on the need of fruit bearing did not leave His disciples in the dark regarding the method and the means for an abundant and immeasurably rich and permanent fruitage. "If ye abide in me and my words abide in you, ye shall ask what ye will, and it shall be done unto you. . . . Ye have not chosen me, but I have chosen you, and ordained you, that ye should go and bring forth fruit, and that your fruit should remain: that whatsoever ye shall ask of the Father in my name, he may give it you" (John 15:7, 16).

We have the Savior's example as it appears in His high priestly prayer, the prayer of intercession (John 17) where He prayed for all who should believe on Him clear across the centuries. "Neither pray I for these alone, but for them also which believe on me through their word." Our Lord's intercession in the upper room with the shadow of the Cross upon Him wiped out time and place and embraced the ages, girdling, as it did, the entire world. All Christians of whatever place or age were embraced.

In the epistles of Paul we see how he followed his Master's example. To the Philippians he writes, saying: "I thank God upon every remembrance of you, always in every prayer of mine for you all making request with joy, for your fellowship in the gospel from the first day until now" (Phil. 1:3, 4). He in prison at Rome, they far away over in Philippi, Greece. To the Colossians he writes: "We give thanks to God and the Father of our Lord Jesus Christ, praying always for you, since we heard of your faith in Christ Jesus, and of the love which ye have to all the saints" (Col.

1:3, 4). Paul in Rome and they in Colossae. "Epaphras, who is one of you," he goes on to say, "a servant of Christ, saluteth you, always labouring fervently for you in prayers, that ye may stand perfect and complete in all the will of God" (Col. 4:12).

Hudson Taylor, the founder of the China Inland Mission, was travelling in the U.S.A. and speaking in different churches in the interests of his mission. In a certain church after speaking, a gentleman approached him to ask questions regarding a certain mission station in China. As Hudson Taylor talked with this gentleman, he was surprised to find that said person was so well acquainted with this station, its needs and problems. Hudson Taylor questioned the gentleman as to why he was so fully informed regarding this mission station. The answer was that when the missionary of this particular station went to the field, they made a solemn agreement. One was to go to China to labor in the field while the other, who stayed at home, was to intercede daily at the throne of grace according to the needs and problems which the missionary would write about, thus keeping his prayer partner informed about the many aspects of the work. Hudson Taylor said to this prayer warrior that he now knew why this particular station was flourishing and achieving as no other station of the mission. Ah yes, it was the ministry of intercession of this dedicated Christian that made the difference.

I was up against a very difficult situation in Argentina some years ago. The fort (if I may put it that way) was held by the enemy, the prince

of the darkness of this world. I prayed and labored
with all the strength I could muster. All to no
avail. Then one day a letter came from a dear
lady who had promised that she would be praying
for me, saying: "Be of good cheer. I have touched
the throne for you." I knew then that victory in
this most difficult situation was to be mine. And
so it was. Shortly after the Lord laid bare His
arm and the fort was gloriously taken for Christ
and His Kingdom.

In the closing years of his life Evan Roberts,
the noted Welsh revivalist, who was so mightily
used of God to bring revival to the churches of
Wales, withdrew from an active participation in
the work of churches to give himself to the ministry
of intercession. There were not a few who pressed
the evangelist to come back into the ministry of
preaching the gospel. But Evan Roberts replied
to all these requests, saying that he was now occupied with the ministry of intercession. His field
of labor was not only Wales but the entire world.
He was interceding for the entire Body of Christ;
the church in all lands was his burden. His scope
now was the world, the spiritual needs of all countries which he would bless through Him who said:
"Call unto me and I will answer thee and show
thee great and mighty things which thou knowest
not." In Ezekiel 22:30, 31, we have the Lord saying:
"And I sought for a man among them, that should
make up the hedge, and stand in the gap before
me for the land, that I should not destroy it; but
I found none. Therefore I have poured out mine
indignation upon them; I have consumed them with
the fire of my wrath; their own way have I recom-

pensed upon their heads, saith the Lord God."

One trembles before such a picture. Can it be, one wonders, that intercession on the part of one of His children may be instrumental in saving a nation? Why should the Lord need intercession on the part of those of His family who know and love Him, so as not to destroy a sinful people? Again we are faced by mystery. I shall not attempt to answer the question. There are theologians better fitted to answer such a question. I prefer to humbly accept this as it comes to us in the pages of Holy Writ, without quibling.

We have an example in the life of Moses, the faithful servant of the Most High. While he was in the mount (Sinai) for forty days and nights, the Israelites corrupted themselves, worshipping the golden calf which Aaron had made, and dancing gleefully about it. The Lord told Moses to descend from the mount and see what was taking place. When he beheld this horrible scene of idolatry, in anger he broke the tables of stone which the Lord had given him and exclaimed, "Ye have sinned a great sin; and now I will go up to the Lord; peradventure I will make an atonement for your sin."

We read that the Lord said unto Moses, "Now let me alone, that my wrath may wax hot against the people and that I may consume them; and I will make of thee a great nation."

But Moses had learned the holy art of intercession. He knew that the Lord was merciful and gracious and compassionate, though He hated sin and abominated idolatry. Moses returned to the mount to meet the Lord and plead for mercy upon his people. It is well to read the whole story (Exodus 32). The forty days of intercession came to a great climax with Moses exclaiming, "O this people have sinned a great sin, and have made them gods of gold. Yet now, if thou wilt forgive their sin—; and if not, blot me, I pray thee, out of the book which thou hast written." Moses triumphs.

Though some of the leaders perished, the people were spared. "Lead the people," said the Lord, "into the place of which I have spoken unto thee. Behold mine Angel shall go before thee."

Such bold, sacrificial intercession is well pleasing to the Lord. Moses had said, in effect, that if there was no forgiveness for his people, he would perish with them. Such intercession in which Moses was ready to lose all, he being innocent, for the sake of his people, even as the Lord our Savior for the sake of sinful humanity gave up all, identified as He was with the sins of the world; such intercessions, I repeat, is well pleasing to the Father.

How we need to learn the holy art of intercession. Let us give thanks that the Holy Spirit, as we saw in chapter 3, is ready to help our infirmities, which are never greater than when we approach the throne of God; let us give thanks because we are not alone in this sublime ministry. The Holy Spirit, who maketh intercession for us with groanings which cannot be uttered, helps our infirmities. He will draw us out in prayer and show us what to pray for. Our joy will be unspeakable and full of glory, as Peter puts it in his first epistle, and great shall be the blessings received.

CHAPTER VII

INTERCESSION THROUGH PRAISE

Intercession is a two-way street. I speak to God. God speaks to me. It would be better to put God first. He speaks to me; I speak to Him. "My sheep," says the Savior, "hear my voice."

There is nothing that makes intercession so effective as praise. We see it in the Psalms. How the voice of praise resounds through the Psalms. The Psalmist is forever praising the Lord. "I will praise thee, O Lord my God, with all my heart" (Ps. 86:12). In Psalm 104:33 he says: "I will sing unto the Lord as long as I live: I will sing praise to my God as long as I live." In Psalm 103:1-5, we find him exclaiming, "Bless the Lord, O my soul: and all that is within me, bless his holy name. Bless the Lord, O my soul, and forget not all his benefits. Who forgiveth all thine iniquities, who healeth all thy diseases: who redeemeth thy life from destruction; who crowneth thee with lovingkindness and tender mercies; who satisfieth thy mouth with good things; so that thy youth is renewed like the eagles." In Psalm 139:14, this sweet singer of Israel rejoices, saying: "I will praise thee; for I am fearfully and wonderfully made: marvellous are thy works; and that my soul knoweth right well."

In Psalm 146 the Psalmist, with his usual joy,

lifts his voice saying: "Praise ye the Lord. Praise the Lord, O my soul. While I live I will praise the Lord: I will sing praises to my God while I have any being." In Psalm 147, the Psalmist declares, saying, "Praise ye the Lord: for it is good to sing praises unto our God: for it is pleasant, and praise is comely." In Psalm 108 he goes on to say, "O God, my heart is fixed; I will sing and give praise, even with my glory.... I will praise thee, O Lord, among the people; and I will sing praises unto thee among the nations."

In Psalm 113 we read: "Praise ye the Lord. Praise, O ye servants of the Lord, praise the name of the Lord. Blessed be the name of the Lord from this time forth, and forever more. From the rising of the sun unto the going down of the same, the Lord's name is to be praised."

In the closing Psalm (150) it is all praise: "Praise ye the Lord. Praise God in his sanctuary: praise him in the firmament of his power. Praise him for his mighty acts: praise him according to his excellent greatness. Praise him with the sound of a trumpet: praise him with the psaltery and harp. Praise him with timbrel and dance: praise him with stringed instruments and organs. Praise him upon the loud cymbals: praise him upon the high sounding cymbals. Let everything that hath breath praise the Lord. Praise ye the Lord."

As we read the Psalms, we see that whatever the circumstances, in joy or in sorrow, in want or in plenty, in adversity or in prosperity, the order of the day is praise. Some years ago a young lady missionary from China visited us in

Mexico. She was a very joyous, triumphant Christian. It was my responsibility to interpret for her in a number of churches of the country. So I was in a position to observe this missionary and note carefully her manner of life. All day long and in every circumstance it was: "Praise the Lord." At that time I thought it was somewhat overdone. But I have since learned that the Christian, come what may, cannot praise the Lord enough. Though it be night and day with every beat of the heart, still more praise should be voiced.

The chief point that I want to make in this chapter is that intercession becomes effective praise. Praise keeps the channel clear. The hindrances that would hold up the blessings, which our intercessions would bring from the throne of grace are swept away. The rubbish which our secret self-love, our unholy bent toward self, is wont to engender, is removed. Praise is the acknowledgment that no matter what our petty condition may be, God is infinitely good and to be praised at all times.

There is nothing that so draws the Father of lights to the Christian (the Christian who has surrendered to Christ and has crowned Him Lord of his life) as praise. There is nothing which so effectively draws the Lord and makes it possible for Him to work as praise. We are told in Psalm 22 that the Lord inhabits the praises of Israel. Praise creates the atmosphere necessary for the Holy Spirit to manifest Himself and to fulfill His appointed office.

It stands to reason that no one wants to come

home from his day's labor only to find his wife and children sad, and grouchy, and grumbling, and bitter, quarreling and pouting over this and that. With what joy does he come home, hastening his step, knowing that the house will be full of cheer, and laughter, and love and song. The Holy Spirit, by whom the Lord manifests Himself to the believer, dwelling in his heart and life, is grieved, if not quenched, where there is a sour, grouchy, heavyhearted, grumbling spirit. He inspires—as is seen in Galatians 5:22-23—love, joy, peace, longsuffering, gentleness, goodness, faith, meekness, temperance. The sweet music of praise adorns the heart of the believer who walks even as Jesus walked.

Let it be clearly understood that praise is comely, not only when all goes well, according to our deepest longings, but also when we are sorely tried; yea, in the midst of a fiery trial. "Beloved, think it not strange concerning the fiery trial which is to try you, as though some strange thing happened unto you: but rejoice inasmuch as ye are partakers of Christ's sufferings; that, when his glory shall be revealed, ye may be glad also with exceeding joy" (I Pet. 4:12-13).

It was at midnight in a dank prison cell, with their backs bloody from the scourging they had received, that Paul and Silas sang hymns of praise (Acts 16:25). Little wonder that an earthquake from the Lord shook the prison, freeing the inmates from their chains. What would have happened if instead of praise Paul and Silas had given way to murmurings and grumblings and heavyhearted complaints? I shall leave it to the reader to say.

Every trial has a blessing hidden away in its bosom. How clearly this is manifested in the life of Joseph. Sold into slavery by his brothers who hated him, falsely accused by his master's wife and cast into prison, he keeps sweet, looking after his fellow prisoners. It was all a prelude and a preparation for the high honor that would be bestowed upon him. He becomes the highest in the realm after Pharaoh. It was he who gave food to the hungry multitudes not only of Egypt but of other lands during the seven years of drought. Behold, how the brothers, who had hated him and sold him into slavery, come and prostrate themselves at his feet in search of corn that they and their father might not die of hunger.

Mark tell us (14:26) that our Lord, who in all things is our example, after the celebration of the Passover and the institution of the Communion Supper, went out into the Mount of Olives, singing a psalm of praise. He was on the way to Gethsemane and Calvary. He went singing.

How it moves and fires one with a solemn resolution to "count it all joy, when ye fall into divers temptations; knowing this, that the trying of your faith worketh patience" (James 1:2-3).

CHAPTER VIII

INTERCESSION—
A SUBLIME ADVENTURE

There are no joys, no thrills like those which the intercessor experiences. His joy is unspeakable and full of glory. He reaches into the bank of heaven and bestows such riches upon mankind, riches of a celestial nature, as no prince or millionaire could ever give. He believes his Lord's word—namely, that whatsoever he may ask of the Father in the Name of Jesus, it shall be given. And so he opens his hand and, via the throne of grace, blesses souls far and near as no philanthropist has ever been able to do.

At one time when I was preaching in Cuba and teaching in one of the seminaries of that land, I had come to the end of my physical and spiritual resources. Sunday came, but I was sick and planning to stay in bed. A voice from downstairs called: "There is someone here who wants to see you." So I dressed (much to my dislike) and went to see who it was. Lo and behold, it was a young black girl who spoke up at once and said: "I have come to pray for you." Was I willing? Indeed I was. God had sent the frail little figure, a maid of perhaps fifteen years.

We went out on a great rock where my friend

knelt to pray. Never have I heard such a prayer. The heavens opened at the voice of this black girl. When she finished I was a new man: healed, spiritually and physically. I was ready, equipped for anything.

There is nothing too small or too great for the Father of lights not to hear and work the wonders that He alone can do in answer to believing intercession. The hairs of our head are numbered, not a sparrow falls without the knowledge of the Father. Mountains of difficulty do move when the Christian bows the knee and calls upon the Father.

In the days of World War I, General Allenby, in charge of the British Forces in Egypt, was ordered to move northward and take Jerusalem. Turkey at that time, possessor of the Holy Land, was an ally of Germany. When the general reached Jerusalem it befell him like the Crusaders of old. He trembled and said to his aide, "I can't bomb the Holy City. What shall we do?" Allenby, a Christian, called the officers of his staff and put the problem before them. Would they join him in intercession asking the Lord to intervene? They said they would. Behold the British general with his officers on their knees calling upon the Lord to show His hand so that the Holy City might not be bombed. The result? Did God work a miracle? Indeed He did. As morning dawned a man came forth from Jerusalem with a white flag to surrender the city, which was taken without a shot being fired.

Let us move to a yet greater mountain of difficulty. A book entitled *God Was At Dunkirk* tells the story. The Maginot line of fortresses had fallen in World War II and France was taken. The British Forces were fleeing before the German "Wermacht." Hitler was laughing gleefully. The British army would be stopped at the channel where he would overtake the Tommies and annihilate them.

George the Sixth, seeing the peril, issued a decree calling Britons throughout the empire to call on the almighty God to intervene in that hour, the most critical of the war. The result? A storm over Germany so terrible that not a finger, so to speak, could move, while on the channel a stillness that left the waters as smooth as glass. Britons had never seen the channel so smooth. All day ships plied back and forth—warships, small fishing boats, men and women crossing the channel to rescue the troops. There were 370,000 soldiers rescued. Military leaders have said that at Dunkirk the tide of war turned. Hitler met his Waterloo at Dunkirk. British soldiers met in groups to thank the Lord for his intervention, saving Britain as He did.

The limit of the power of intercession is nothing more nor less than the limit of divine resources. "Call unto me and I will answer thee and show thee great and mighty things that thou knowest not" (Jer. 33:3) still stands. Truly, intercession is a sublime adventure.

But we must not think that it is only the great affairs of the nations which are of interest to the Lord. There is no phase of life that does not interest Him. Home, the children, school, business, governments—all is grist for the mill of intercession. Of course prayer has laws that must be heeded. Those laws are the theme of my book, *Prayer's Deeper Secrets*. I do not want to repeat what has been said. It may all be summed up in one sentence: We must walk with Jesus in humble obedience. If He says no to a petition of ours, we may be sure that He has something much better in store for us. We had an answer. A no from the Most High, coming as it does from Him, the infinitely adorable one, is in itself a sublime answer.

I had been away preaching. Upon my return, the good wife met me at the door saying, "I am so glad you have come. Johnny needs you." I hastened upstairs and found our boy, then nine years old, pitching around in bed with an unbearable earache. I drew near and said one word. It is found in Luke 7:7 where the Roman centurion said to Jesus, "Say in a word and my servant shall be healed." "Speak the word, Lord," is all I said. Our boy fell asleep at once. He awoke in the morning without a pain. I felt that this was my opportunity to lead Johnny to a definite commitment to Christ. "Don't you think, Johnny, that out of gratitude you ought now to give yourself to Jesus?" Yes, he did. It was done. He is now a missionary of the Cross in old Mexico.

LeTourneau, the well-known Christian who has invented so many bulldozers of one kind and another, has testified that when he is inventing a machine and comes to a point where he is baffled not knowing what the next step should be, he bows his head in prayer. Whereupon the Lord gives him the key.

Peter, the apostle, was in prison. Prayer was

made without ceasing by the church unto God for him (Acts 12:5). "The angel of the Lord came upon him and a light shined in the prison: and he smote Peter on the side, and raised him up, saying, Arise up quickly. And his chains fell off from his hands. And the angel said unto him, Gird thyself, and bind on thy sandals. . . . Cast thy garment about thee and follow me" (Acts 5:7, 8). The gates of the prison opened of their own accord. Peter "wist not that it was true which was done by the angel; but thought he saw a vision," as the Sacred Scripture reads. But it was not a vision. It was hard facts. Peter was free.

The only reason why we do not have sublime adventures in the realm of intercession, facing up to the problems all about us, is that we do not take the Lord seriously where He says, "Ask and ye shall receive, seek and ye shall find, knock and it shall be opened unto you. . . . What things soever ye desire when ye pray, believe that ye receive them and ye shall have them" (Mark 11: 24).

All this is a challenge for us to enter the ministry of intercession. Sublime adventures await us. We will soon be holding our breath in utter amazement as we see the Lord at work in our behalf. The school of intercession has many lessons for us to learn. Ours will be a growing faith and wisdom. The Lord will lovingly and patiently teach us until we come to the stature of a disciple able to grapple with problems more and more difficult.

Henry Milans had reached the top in his profession as a writer. One evening with friends he tasted liquor for the first time in his life. It surprised him. He liked it. It was the beginning of a downgrade unfolding of his life. He became a drunkard. He stuck to the bottle and lost all, living like a drowned rat in an underground passage in New York for two years.

One evening he heard a Salvation Army officer on one of the street corners of the great metropolis. That same night he knelt beside the drum and accepted Christ as his Savior. Henry was transformed. His chain was broken. He reached the top of his profession once more. Shortly after his conversion he went to tell his aged mother what had happened. You can imagine her joy. "Henry," she said, "I knew you would come to the Lord and be saved. I prayed for you every day. I knew that the Lord would save you." Intercession is the most sublime of all adventures.

CHAPTER IX

WATCHMEN UPON THY WALLS

In the book of the prophet Isaiah chapter 62:6-7, we find these words: "I have set watchmen upon thy walls, O Jerusalem, which shall never hold their peace day nor night: ye that make mention of the Lord, keep not silence, and give him no rest, till he establish, and till he make Jerusalem a praise in the earth."

What a strange admonition this is. It is the Lord speaking. We are to give Him no rest day or night. He had placed intercessors upon the walls of Jerusalem who were told to "keep not silence," to give Him no rest till He had made Jerusalem a praise in the earth.

We can hardly understand this. We who are parents so often wish that our children would leave us in peace. We grow weary because of their nagging over something which they want.

However, it is not so with the Lord. On the contrary, He bids us give Him no rest day or night as we intercede for the church, for our friends, for needy souls, for whatever He may have burdened us with. In Psalm 121 we are told that the Lord neither slumbers nor sleeps: "He that keepeth thee will not slumber." We are to press our claims in earnest intercession until the answer is given. This is faith.

There is often a delay. But on the other hand, as we see in the book of the prophet Isaiah, before we call, the blessing which we seek is given.

As a missionary on the foreign field, I have known, intimately, intercessors who did just this. They were constantly at it day and night. They rejoiced in the Lord with joy unspeakable and full of glory (I Pet. 1:8). They laid hold of the promises of the Lord and pressed their claims until the desired blessing was bestowed.

The missionary goes to the field to teach and preach Jesus Christ. However, it frequently happens that the missionary's children (perhaps I should say converts) often outstrip him, achieving higher heights and deeper depths of faith and love in Christ the Lord. They unconsciously become the teachers, while the missionary is the one who is taught. I have in mind two such intercessors whom I looked upon as my teachers in the school of the holy art of intercession.

General Curti, a retired officer of the Mexican army, was brought to the Lord through a dream in which he saw Jesus the Lord. No one could claim him as a convert inasmuch as his conversion came right out of heaven like the apostle Paul. One could not doubt the validity of the general's conversion in view of the achievements of this man of God, and the consistency of his life as a Christian.

It was while he was still a colonel that the vision which brought him to Christ took place. Some time prior he was in hot country and came down with a consuming fever. The army physician attending the colonel said that it would be necessary to get him out of the hot country, and that it could only be done by packing him in ice. But there was no ice to be had. What were they to do? It looked hopeless.

It was then, according to the colonel's testimony, that a cloud appeared with an abundance of hail falling to the ground. The hail was gathered up in bags and so the colonel was packed in ice and taken from the scene. During the journey the ice gave out. There was need of more ice. Again the cloud appeared with hail falling to the ground, and so the colonel was freshly packed in ice and carried to cooler altitudes where he recovered shortly.

When the colonel gave this testimony in a downtown church in Mexico City, I was present. An officer who accompanied the colonel at the time of his illness arose and said, "I can vouch for the truth of this testimony, for I was present when it took place."

Shortly after his recovery Curti, now a general, had the wondrous dream of which we have spoken which brought him to Christ. He says that for three days he paced the floor saying to himself, "I can't surrender to Christ, I'm an army officer. There is no place for these things in the army." It was then that a text was given to him who had never read the Bible. "Be of good cheer, I have overcome the world." With this the colonel came to me and asked for baptism. He and his wife were baptized and received into the church. One does not wonder that Curti believes in the doctrine of election. He knows that he was chosen and cared for before he ever knew Christ.

The general is a man who lives in a constant spirit of intercession. He has never had any theological training, yet he excels in the holy art of soul winning.

Some time ago I received a telegram from Curti, requesting that I meet him at the depot. He was then the head of the military prison in Saltillo. I met my brother and took him out to the house. He said that due to an error in the timing of his arrival, he was not taken immediately to the military prison at Mexico City. I was told that he was accused of a misappropriation of funds. He had used army funds to buy Bibles for the prisoners. He felt that Bibles were more necessary than bread or shoes. The military judges would never understand that.

Curti was much in prayer. As he left the house the following morning to present himself before the military authority, he asked me to put him in the Lord's hand, which I did.

At noon the general appeared, all aglow, to tell me how the Lord had wrought his deliverance. Sitting beside the judge as he (Curti) entered the office was an old friend of his, General Rico, with whom Curti had dealt in an effort to bring him to Christ. General Rico arose and embraced Curti and, turning to the judge, said: "Mr. Judge, let me present to you my friend, a man without sin [impeccable as it is in Spanish]." That was the end of accusations against the colonel. His prayer was wonderfully answered. I have seen a picture of the Sunday School which the colonel formed in the military prison at Saltillo, each man with his Bible.

When the colonel was in charge of the quartel at Merida, Yucatan, a general appeared from Mexico City saying they would have a shooting trial the day following. Curti's heart sank. He had not fired a shot for nine years. He thought, "I'll be the poorest shot of the bunch and be laughed at by the very men I have sought to win for Christ. They will say, 'There you have it. When it comes to something practical these Christians are no good.'"

The colonel went home and gave himself to intercession. Shortly after, he appeared before his wife and asked her to keep the children quiet, as the Lord had spoken to him and given him peace. The next day he met with his fellow officers for the shooting trial. To the amazement of all, the colonel shot the bullet straight through the bull's eye. The general stepped forward and ran his pencil through the hole. He could hardly believe what he saw. He gave the colonel a new assignment as a rifle instructor. The Lord Jesus was glorified and Curti was joyful, triumphant.

Some few years ago I was speaking to pastors and students in a village near Oaxaca. I was overcome with joy as I was given liberty and power such as I had never experienced before. When the meeting was over I was taken to a chicken coup at the rear of the Bible Institute. There was a young man giving himself to intercession. Ezekiel Contreras, a student of the Institute, I was told, had entered the ministry of intercession. I was often with this Spirit-anointed young man in the years that followed and was in a position to observe his manner of life. Ezekiel has come to be a mighty prayer-warrior. When he is present at a Bible conference or a series of evangelistic gatherings, or meetings aimed at revival in the church, great things are wrought not because of any eloquence of the speakers, but simply because Ezekiel Contreras has entered the ministry of intercession. He gives the Lord no rest until the heavens are opened and the Spirit of God takes over.

CHAPTER X

FEAR NOT—ONLY BELIEVE

The point where intercession often breaks down and fails to achieve what may be wrought thereby is where prayer ends and faith begins. If we are sensitive to the Spirit's direction, we shall know when to cease interceding and simply believe. In a very real sense it is easier to intercede than to believe. While we are interceding we have confidence that the blessing we earnestly desire will be given. But when we are no longer praying it comes to pass only too frequently that we fail to maintain an attitude of real faith.

Let us turn to the Word and see this factor as it appears in the ministry of our Lord.

In the gospel according to St. Matthew the ninth chapter beginning at the 27th verse, we have the story of the two blind men to whom Jesus gave sight. We read that they followed the Lord crying and saying, "Thou son of David, have mercy on us." We must note what Jesus said to these unfortunate men. "Believe ye that I am able to do this?" They said unto Him, "Yea Lord." We read that then Jesus touched their eyes saying, "According to your faith be it unto you." And their eyes were opened.

We plainly see here that prayer is not enough. As we cease interceding, there comes the trial of faith. Then is when we must hold the ground, so to speak, and maintain an attitude of unwavering confidence. The enemy will make an effort, yea, not one but many, to undermine our faith. He will laugh at us for presuming to believe what we cannot see. He will mock us as silly mortals for believing that such a difficult thing will come to pass.

Years ago there fell into my hands a tract in which the writer maintained that many blessings for which we plead at the throne of grace do not materialize because the door of expectation is not kept open. The Lord comes with the gift, but we are not expecting such a blessed thing. In other words, we have earnestly interceded, but we have not maintained an abiding faith that the blessing sought shall be granted. To the two blind men who cried after Jesus that He might give them sight came the searching reply, "Believe ye that I am able to do this?"

In Matthew's gospel chapter 15, we have the story of the Canaanite woman who cried tearfully after Jesus to undertake in her behalf as her daughter was grievously vexed with a devil. The Lord answered her not a word. The disciples, not understanding the Master's silence, thinking that He simply would not heed the woman's cry because she, a Canaanite, was beyond the pale of Judaism, said, "Send her away; for she crieth after us." When Jesus spoke it was to discourage the woman even more, "I am not sent but unto the lost sheep of the house of Israel."

We read, however, that the woman ceased not to cry, saying, "Lord, help me." She was not to be daunted. She continued to press her case. Then came a yet more severe test of her faith as the Lord turned to her and said, "It is not meet to take the children's bread, and to cast it to dogs." Ah, what a test of the woman's faith was this. Would she give up, or would she continue to hope? Would she be able to look beyond such contrary circumstances and believe, despite the rebuke? Her reply won the day. There could not be found words more pleasing to the Lord who said, "O woman, great is thy faith, be it unto thee as thou wilt." Whereupon we read that the demon-possessed daughter was made whole from that very hour.

It was all a test of faith. And so our faith shall be tested. There will be seemingly no answer to our cry. Matters may even grow worse. Will we be able to keep the door of expectancy open? We may have to wait many days before the answer to our intercessions brings from heaven the desired result. Or it may be, as it is in the book of Isaiah chapter 65 verse 24, where the Lord says, "While they are yet speaking, I will hear." However it may be, faith must hold to the very end when the shout of victory may be given.

In the same chapter of Isaiah's prophecy, we read in verse 4 the following words, "Since the beginning of the world men have not heard, nor perceived by the ear, neither hath the eye seen, O God, beside thee what he hath prepared for him that waiteth for him." Sometimes we often have to wait patiently with the door of expectation wide open until faith is crowned with success.

In the gospel according to St. Mark, chapter 11, verse 24, we have the Lord saying, "What things soever ye desire, when ye pray, believe that ye receive them, and ye shall have them." Here again faith is underscored. We must believe, otherwise we might as well forego interceding.

To Jairus, the ruler of the synagogue, whose 12-year-old daughter lay dying, Jesus responded by following the good man to his house (Luke 8:41). We read that he fell down at Jesus' feet. Such a faith and such a need could not but elicit a loving response from the Master. But on the way people thronged Him and other needs came under Jesus' care, so much so that meanwhile the girl died. One from the ruler's house came saying it would be better not to trouble the Master as the child was now dead. Now when Jesus heard it, He turned to Jairus and said, "Fear not: only believe and she shall be made whole."

Upon arriving at the ruler's house, our Lord silenced the mourners saying, "Weep not, she is not dead but sleepeth." They laughed Him to scorn, knowing that the girl was dead. The Lord put all the mourners out, and took her by the hand and said, "Maid, arise," and her spirit came again and she arose.

How very precious are the words "Fear not, only believe." Matters got worse when the ruler appealed to Jesus. But he was not to look at circumstances; he was to hold on and not give way to fear. Intercessors sorely need this, for fear is ever at the door knocking. However contrary circumstances may seem, they are bidden not to fear but to remain steadfast, believing, knowing that their faith will at last be crowned with the laurels of victory.

In the epistle of James we come upon this very pertinent admonition, "If any of you lack wisdom, let him ask of God, that giveth to all men liberally, and upbraideth not; and it shall be given him. But let him ask in faith, nothing wavering. For he that wavereth is like a wave of the sea driven with the wind and tossed. For let not that man think that he shall receive anything of the Lord" (James 1:5-7). "Fear not, only believe. . . . Lord, I believe, help thou mine unbelief."

CHAPTER XI

INTERCESSION'S
SUPREME MOTIVE

Some years ago I was wont to drop into a church to take part in a midweek gathering for prayer. It surprised me greatly to hear the pastor saying as he prayed, "Lord, forgive our prayers." I thought, "How very strange; if there is one thing holy it is prayer." But as the years have passed after much experience in the art of intercession, I have come to understand. Yes, we need to ask the Lord to forgive us for the way, at times, we pray.

There is such a thing as evil praying. We find the Biblical authority for such a statement in James 4:3, where the sacred writer declares, "Ye ask, and receive not, because ye ask amiss, that ye may consume it upon your lusts."

Jesus, our Lord, said as much when He replied to James and John, who had requested the first place in the kingdom of God, "Ye know not what ye ask." In Romans 8:26, the apostle Paul states that we know not what we should pray for as we ought.

I used to think that, if there is one thing the devil cannot touch, it is our prayers. I have changed my mind. The devil does meddle with our prayers. He is never so gleeful as when he gets us to intercede with a mistaken zeal, a mistaken end, and wrong motive. Even in such a holy thing as a confession of sins, the enemy is wont to show his hand, for Satan always hides and works under counterfeits of good things. Beware of a confession of sins which may be made because of the accusations of evil spirits. When they are at work bringing to mind passed sins, instead of a relief of one's conscience, matters get worse. The harder one prays the blacker the sin appears and the more discouraged one becomes. When it is the real working of the Holy Spirit who convicts of sin, then confession brings immediate relief and there is joy and peace and freedom.

Now this brings us to the question of the right motive in intercession. There are many motives in all that we do. It may be the lust for money, it may be ambition for high office in government, it may be the desire to shine in social circles, it may be an aim to appear more devoted to God than is really the case, it may be a young man's purpose to appear more noble than he really is, in the eyes of the maid he loves, it may be a lust for power, it may be an aim to beat the other fellow in business. Indeed, there is a great diversity of motives that inspire men and drive them to action. Now these are all right in their place. We are not saying that they are all bad.

What I am getting at is that a wrong motive in prayer can be disastrous. Here, too, a diversity of motives are behind our intercessions. If we have not been thoroughly purified, we will be asking amiss, as James puts it, that we may consume it upon our lusts. It is one thing to be actuated with a holy desire that God might be glorified; it is a horse of another color, as we say, for one to pray with nothing but selfish ends in view.

If intercession is to achieve and bring the great blessings that we are told in Holy Writ or may be brought to bear upon suffering humanity, then we must have as our end nothing less than the glory of God. This may seem at first flush an impossible thing. How can we rise above the purely human way of thinking and acting when the self-life (Paul calls it the flesh) is so very strong in every one of us? How am I to intercede before the throne of grace, having as the all-consuming passion of my heart and mind that God might be glorified? He says that He will not give His glory to another.

The answer is found in the Cross. We come back to what was said in a foregoing chapter. In God's plan and thought the Christian is identified with his Lord. When his Lord was crucified, he was crucified; when his Lord arose from the grave, he arose. The Christian is more than conqueror through Him who loved him. It is the function of the Holy Spirit to apply what has been called the "radium of the Cross." The cancer of our secret "self-love" can be removed only by an application of the power of the Cross in an ever more complete manner. Whereupon, what Scripture calls "the new man" will appear. The "new man" in a perfectly natural and spontaneous way is fired with a holy zeal whose end is the glory of God.

When our Lord cleansed the temple at Jerusalem, which had become a den of thieves, it wasn't that He simply desired to see the house of God cleansed. No! The zeal of His Father's house had eaten Him up. "Make not my Father's house a house of merchandise." It was the glory of the Father which was at stake. "I have glorified thee on the earth," said Jesus in His high priestly prayer.

When the motive of the intercessor is the glory of God, then it becomes possible to move mountains. There is no limit then to the power of prayer except the power and wisdom of God, which are without limit. If we will stand upon the ground of Calvary, we can laugh at difficulties and the impossible is easily accomplished. If we can say, as we intercede for some need in home or church or school or government, "Father, that thou mightest be glorified," we shall most certainly receive what we ask for.

An amazing thing took place in the Olympics held in the University Stadium of Mexico City last year. A young man who had won in one of the races, as he dashed through to victory, got down on his knees before a vast throng of spectators and gave thanks to God. When asked why he had done that, his reply was that he had prayed for victory and now wanted to give God the glory. You do not wonder that his prayer was heard.

There is a striking example in the Old Testament of intercession crowned with the laurels of victory, because the intercessors were actuated by the right motive. Hezekiah was king of Judah. It was in the days of Isaiah the prophet. Sennacherib, king of Assyria, had come up against Jerusalem with a vast host of soldiers to take the

Holy City. Rab-shakeh, Sennacherib's general in charge of the king's army, stood close to the walls of the city and blasphemed the God of Israel.

"Let not thy God in whom thou trustest deceive thee," so cried Rab-shakeh, saying, "Jerusalem shall not be delivered into the hand of the king of Assyria. Behold, thou hast heard what the kings of Assyria have done to all lands by destroying them utterly: and shalt thou be delivered? Have the gods of the nations delivered them which my fathers have destroyed; as Gozan, and Haran, and Rezeph, and the children of Eden which were in Thelasar?"

It is a thrilling story. You will find it in chapter 19 of II Kings and chapter 32 of II Chronicles.

King Sennacherib writes a blasphemous letter to Hezekiah calling upon him to surrender. "And Hezekiah received the letter of the hand of the messengers, and read it: and Hezekiah went up into the house of the Lord, and spread it before the Lord. And Hezekiah prayed before the Lord, and said, O Lord God of Israel, which dwellest between the cherubims, thou art the God, even thou alone of all the kingdoms of the earth; Lord, bow down thine ear, and hear: open, Lord, thine eyes, and see: and hear the words of Sennacherib, which hath sent him [Rab-shakeh] to reproach the living God. Of a truth, Lord, the kings of Assyria have destroyed the nations and their lands, and have cast their gods into the fire: for they were no gods, but the work of men's hands, wood and stone, therefore they have destroyed them."

"Now therefore, O Lord our God, I beseech thee, save thou us out of his hand, that all the kingdoms of the earth may know that thou art the Lord God, even thou only."

Hezekiah did not pray for deliverance that the people might enjoy peace, or simply that Judah might be saved. His motive was of higher order. It was, in effect, that the Lord, the God of Israel, might be glorified, that all the nations might know that He alone is God, even He only.

And the Lord sent an angel which cut off all the mighty men of valour and the leaders and captains in the camp of the king of Assyria. So he returned with shame of face to his own land. And when he came into the house of his god, they that came forth of his own bowels (two of his sons), slew him there with the sword.

Ah yes, when the intercessor has as his motive the glory of God, there is no measuring the power of his prayer.

"Lord, teach us to pray," said the disciples of Jesus.

Lord, teach *us*, in this modern age when war, and greed, and violence and wickedness, rampant as never before in the annals of history, threatens the very life of the nations; Lord, teach us to intercede with no other motive than Thy glory.

CHAPTER XII

MORE THAN CONQUERORS

One hesitates to say what I am about to affirm; it is so very apparent. I refer to the times in which we live; they are so very perilous.

"This know," wrote St. Paul to Timothy, his son in the faith, "that in the last days perilous times shall come" (II Tim. 3:1).

Many signs indicate that we are rapidly moving toward the end of the age. Among these signs the most evident of all is Jerusalem. The Lord had told His disciples that Jerusalem would be trodden down of the Gentiles until the times of the Gentiles should be fulfilled (Luke 21:24). Jerusalem is no longer trodden down. She has surged again from the ruins of the past to become a nation among the nations of the world. She sends her representative to the councils of the United Nations at New York as do other nations of the world. Who would have dreamed that Israel, scattered as she was over the face of the earth, would gather her children from the four quarters of the globe to bring to life once more a nation which had ceased to exist for so many centuries? The Lord said it would be so, and so it is (Luke 21:24).

The Master rebuked the Pharisees and the Sadducees for not being able to discern the signs of the times. "O ye hypocrites," said He, "ye can discern the face of the sky; but cannot discern the signs of the times." It was the signs of the Savior's advent, which so many miracles had heralded, that these bigoted Pharisees failed to see. The signs of the second advent, which are so very apparent, are not observed, not because they are not evident, but because of the hypocrisy of believers in our day.

Men's hearts, said the Lord, would fail them for fear of those things which would come to pass (Matt. 21:26). Iniquity would abound, and because of this the love of many would wax cold (Matt. 24:12).

Iniquity in our day is taking on forms never known in all the annals of history. Two world wars have brought a flood of demons upon mankind. In the ninth chapter of the Apocalypse, St. John, the seer of Patmos, tells us that there would come a time when the bottomless pit would be opened, out from which would come smoke as a great furnace and that the sun and the air would be darkened by reason of the smoke from the pit. He identifies the locusts which emanate as horses with the faces of men and tails like unto scorpions. He evidently, under a figurative language, is speaking of demons, for he goes on to say that they had as their king one whose name in the Hebrew tongue is Abaddon and in the Greek tongue Appollyon. Since he is king of the bottomless pit, the reference is without doubt to the devil.

Indeed, the times in which we are living are most perilous. Our universities have become the battleground where the youth of our day, stirred up by alien forces, are at war with the existing order.

It is all a call to Christians to buckle on the armour of God and stand against the devil. There is but one force that can withstand the flood of wickedness from the pit and drive out these evil spirits which as smoke from a great furnace envelop the nations. Behind the manifest wickedness of our times are the rulers of the darkness of this world. The whole world lieth in the power of the wicked one, John tells us in his first epistle (5:19).

Again, I repeat, there is only one weapon that can deal with these dark spirits. That weapon is intercessory prayer.

How great is the need in these times, so very, very perilous, for an army of prayer warriors strong enough in faith to challenge these awful powers of darkness and overthrow the strongholds of the wicked one. Let us not be deceived. We do not wrestle against flesh and blood, as Paul writes to the Ephesians, but against principalities and powers and against the rulers of the darkness of this world.

In Ephesians 6, where this awful fact appears, the apostle writes saying that "we are to pray always with all prayer and supplication in the Spirit and watching thereunto with all perserverance and supplication for all saints" (Eph. 6:18).

This brings me to my point in this final chapter on intercession.

To be more than conquerors in this world of woe whose prince is the evil one, we must be sure that no weapon is lacking in our armour. For if there is, we will sooner or later find that the enemy will become cognizant of the fact and attack us along the line of this weak point, where our armour is deficient, and will cause us to go down in shameful defeat.

You will recall, kind reader, that the Savior, with the shadow of the Cross upon Him, remarked saying, "The prince of this world cometh and hath nothing in me" (John 14:30). "Now is the judgment of this world: now shall the prince of this world be cast out" (John 12:31).

It was through the Cross that our Lord triumphed and stripped the enemy of his authority. There is only one ground on which we may triumph. That is Calvary. And we are more than conquerors only as we stand firm on this ground. If we move away from this center (and we may be sure that the enemy will use every means possible, every wile to entice us away from the Cross); if we are drawn away, I repeat, where with Christ we die to ourselves, the enemy will most certainly find ground on which to oppress and defeat us.

We must be stripped of pride and a secret self-love, or the wily foe will lay hold of our pride and trip us up, for there is an affinity between "the flesh," as Paul calls the self life, and the devil. It is ground propitious for his working.

Now to hold this ground where we are one with Christ in death and resurrection, we must be ever on our guard, watching and praying. "Watch and pray," said the Master to His disciples. Here intercession becomes, as it were, the very life-blood of the faith. It is like the air we breathe. As someone has said, we must breathe in Christ and breathe out self.

Armed with the weapon of intercession, we cast

off the powers of darkness. We are now able to exercise authority and give the command of faith in behalf of souls that are bound, the church bogged down by the oppression of the enemy, missions that are in the thick of a conflict with the rulers of the darkness of this world, and so release them from oppression. It may take many days of earnest intercession and valiant wrestling with opposing forces from the pit. If we hold on and do not faint, victory is sure to be ours.

I labored in a country where communism was fast taking over. Children at school were taught to march to the tune of "One, two, there is no god." People were shot down as they came out of church for no other reason than their worship. The atmosphere was unbearably dark and heavy with the powers of darkness in the saddle, so to speak.

What were we to do? A group of pastors and missionaries decided to intercede before the throne of grace each morning at six-thirty, calling upon God to intervene. Some came from an outlying village to join forces with those of the city. The group held on without fail, morning after morning, for six months. The victory of the Cross was applied against the satanic powers that were behind it all.

One morning one of the pastors, all aglow, came in with the morning paper. The president had turned right about face and dismissed the "red" from his cabinet. The atmosphere of the land lifted as when the sun comes out after a storm. The backbone of communism was broken. Years have passed without a serious threat from this quarter.

I have told this story in *Prayer's Deeper Secrets,* but it bears repetition.

So let us trim our lamps of intercession. Let us heed the call to prayer as it is in Jeremiah 33:3, "Call unto me, and I will answer thee, and show thee great and mighty things, which thou knowest not." Let us enter the ministry of intercession. The Lord will lay bare His arm for the overthrow of the strongholds of the wicked one. There will be new life and power in our churches, and barrenness will give way to an era of great fruitfulness, all to the glory of God and His only begotten Son, our Lord Jesus Christ.

OTHER QUALITY BOOKS FROM BETHANY FELLOWSHIP